Loose Horses

PROSE AND POETRY

Jehann El-Bisi

ISBN: 978-1-963565-11-9 (Paperback)

Library of Congress Control Number: 2024907355

Printed in the United States of America

Published by

QUIPPY
QUILL
info@thequippyquill.com
(302) 295-2278

DEDICATION

I dedicate this first book of poetry with love and affection to my son, Elijah Lee El-Bisi. Your unwavering patience is a steady breeze that cools my burning heart. May you always be as honest as birches, in their unmistakable presence in an evergreen grove, and true, so your path will be sure and bright.

Elijah, you are my greatest poem.

In loving memory of Dr. John Bracey, W.E.B. Dubois department of African American Studies, at the University of Massachusetts, of Amherst, who said, "stay in Amherst and write and publish your books." Sadly, he recently passed before I could place this in his hands.

[She] cried the relief she felt at finally seeing the pattern, the way all the stories fit together—the old stories, the war stories, their stories—to become the story that was still being told. [She] was not crazy; [she] had never been crazy. [She] had only seen and heard the world as it always was: no boundaries, only transitions through all distances and time.
-Leslie Marmon Silko

You may write me down in history with your bitter twisted lies. You may trod me in the very dirt, but still, like dust, I'll rise, does my sassiness upset you? ...Did you want to see me broken? .... Does my haughtiness offend you? (laughing) Don't take it awful hard just cause I laugh, (laughing.)
-Maya Angelou from her poem Still I Rise

Maybe that's what souls are for, to take the hurt the heart can't take.
-John Trudell

If we live for their acceptance, we will die from their rejection.
-Lecrae

ACKNOWLEDGEMENTS

Ahéhee' sukrin, kûtaputaush, wopila, arigato, thank you...
Jesus, Creator, Grandfather, Grandmother, Great Spirit...
Tó' éé íínd
Mní W'Coni

Ancestors, African, European and Indigenous...
Mom and Dad (biological parents Dr. Mohamed El-Bisi and Elizabeth Leigh Searle)
Elijah El-Bisi and Isabella Wang
Leila Gordon, Kemal, Karim, and Tarek El-Bisi, Nadia and Gary Graham
Amanda Leigh von Schilling
Constance Jean Albrite
Adoptive Mom-Joan Tavares Avant, Deer Clan Mother, Mashpee Wampanoag Nation
Lena McElroy, Cree Nation, Edmonton, Canada
Lenny Foster, Diné
Madeleine, Art, Doreen, Josh, Alex, Emmitt, and Miles Desmarais
Lili, Abby, Tessa and Miles Louis Chilson Charlotte Giovenella
Louisa, Skip, Johnny, and Montina Santos
Pamela, "little" Jehann, and Jarrell Kirby
Estelle (Mimi,) Nina, John, Kitty Leland and Wyatt Marshall
Seana, Sky, and Cassandra Sunshine Coughlin Amanda Judd
Renée E. Medley and family
Patricia, Joseph, Tara and Eileen Caffrey
Professors Peg Speas and Andy Barto
Nuns and Monks of Nipponzan Myohoji
Hartley H Hennessey
Timothy Bullock
Nichidatsu Fujii Guru Gi
(Ven.) Gyoway Kato
(Sis.) Clare Carter
(Br.) Towbee
Mary Hynes
Dr. Deirdre Almeida and Mariah American Horse
Professor John Bracey and Ingrid Bracey
Rob Leppzer

Jennifer Fasulo and Mahmood Ketabchi
Pearl, Shaylene, Kelli, John and Angela Kydd
Dennis Banks and many members of the American Indian Movement Yankton
Sioux Nation
The Black Panthers
Charmaine Whiteface
Tiokasin Ghost Horse
Eagle Clan Cree Nation
Diné Nation
Oglala Nation
Chief Brave Bear
Chief Potalany
Chief Arvol Lookinghorse
Standing Rock Nation
Sadhguru and Isha Foundation
Maya
Rebecca, Stephanie, Catrina, Brandon and Laura Calnan
Diane and Bill Levine
Sabriyah, Zenobia, and Yasmin Brandford, Aisha
Murdaugh and Tammarrah Lindsay-Brandford
Wally Swist
Professor Ron Welburn
Professor Sut Jhally
Dr. Mark Allen
Martín Espada
Professor Sonia Nieto
Professors Theresa and Mark Austin
Mary and Alan Lemoines
Evie Jenkins
Chéli
Jennifer Ire
Lorraine, Audrey, Obadiah and Simon Chaisson-White
Lola, Larry, Alannah, Danielle Bedaw and family
Andrew Larkin
Sebern Fisher
Alan Bachers
Rev. Sarah Buteux
Joás Lemuel Montero,
Catherine Etheridge

Eileen Furey
Jermaine McGiver
Suzie Montero
Kacie
Sherrie Gove
Mike
Christine
Khristoff
Gabe
Lexie
Todd
Kaila
Dave 1
Dave LaRoche
Phil
Ed Starbuck
All my neighbors I love and may have forgotten, you're not, you're in my heart.

Also, my utmost thanks to Josh Anderson and his team for their timely and endless efforts.

Contents

INTRODUCTION

By Jehann El-Bisi Loose

Horses is a reference to a tragic horse accident with my father when I was ten years old.

In exploring the symbolism of loose horses, I discovered that the horse represents our Ego, and attempts to "control loose horses" represents the struggle spiritually between Ego and Spirit and has variances cross-culturally. So, one of the poems is called Loose Horses, in the book, and illustrates my struggle with the traumatic event involving my father, and my Ego.

I wrote that poem in response to recurring nightmares of the incident, manifesting in me trying to "control loose horses" and my exploration into the symbolism and spiritual wrestling with concepts and practice of surrender, first for me in the sweat lodge and pipe ceremonies for initiation, as a young woman, then in Yoga, in Zen Martial Arts training, chanting the Lotus and Heart Sutras, (far more extensively the Lotus Sutra) and in a Christian sense of surrender to Jesus.

Loose horses were a common phenomenon for our family, in Millis, Massachusetts where we lived. I wondered, reflectively later, since our horses got loose far more often than the neighbors' horses, if they were being intentionally let out, due to racism?

1221

In 1221, Genghis Kahn was so enraged over the loss of his favorite grandson Chagatai Khan that he vowed revenge for his death, and for the heavy casualties lost during his siege of Bamyan. Genghis Kahn completely massacred the population of Bamiyan, Afghanistan and many surrounding regions.

"The destruction was so complete, that the Mongols themselves, referred to Bamyan as the City of Sorrows, or City of Woe. Another name for Bamyan, was "The City of Screams" in reference to the cries of its murdered victims.

This led me to meditate on some of the questions that punctuated my exploration into the nature of the origins of my suffering, and how to eliminate that suffering.

What are these threads of resiliency that bind us in the face of destruction, whether historically or presently? What meaning do we make of the manifestations of those images that are destroyed and recreated?

Enduring existences of symbolic representations that are "destroyed," yet cannot be forever extinguished?

What are these shared human impulses to heal, reveal, and remake us, whole, like Kinsukori?

The Japanese practice of repairing broken vases and objects with gold rendering the broken more valuable, more beautiful, than the unbroken. What are the significances of these sites of reconstruction?

The poem: Return of the Bamiyan Buddha, the reconstruction of the Buddha came from my fascination with the light projection of the "Buddha at Bamiyan," destroyed by the Taliban in March 2001, ordered by the Taliban leader Mullah Mohammad Omar, after the Taliban government declared they were "idols." I saw a magazine article depicting the light show.

I was going to call this first collection of poetry 1221, to reference this scaffolding, emanating from the historical destruction of the entire city, in 1221. I was intrigued by the temporary light projection that drew worshippers

3

in droves. I was wondering how we use light to heal our shared wounds, in a Rumi sense, without rumination, rather invigorated with creativity and action.

What are the effects of the reappearances and manifestations of the Buddha? Or other religious symbols destroyed or desecrated during war, as a tool for social destruction of the invaded and suppressed?

In whose minds are "idols" created and destroyed, only to return again and again, like the indomitable human spirit that arises from the ashes of carnage to create the pure land? These bodhisattvas of our centuries past and present, who tug at our sleeves for change.

My scaffolding for the book of poetry is gleaned from these true stories about destruction, resurrection, reconstruction and renewal. I am drawn to stories of survival, transcendence, and the metaphoric body-temple destroyed; like the Buddha at Bamyan, and the spirit driven persistence and continuation of narratives and commitments to rebirth, renewal rebuilding.

I am investigating the "repeating of sins" throughout our collective human history, and how we intervene and interrupt the desecration of human rights and co-create a more harmonious and peace seeking world. I contemplate the individual, a mere dust mote, reflecting larger cosmic, universal, and global struggles for liberation, from domination, from fear, from war. Seekers who seek, and find themselves, together, everywhere, and nowhere.

I was imagining the dissolution of space and time, the spiritual parallel and significance of the re-appearances of the Buddha. The transcendence of space and time, where and when we can all share experience through expanding consciousness. When will we stop the demonization of "religious" icons as weapons of war? What do agnostics and atheists think of these cultural waves of religious and cultural spiritual inclinations and manifestations?

 Paradoxically, and similarly, what is happening now globally, in scrambles for scarce resources; the same yearning for, and constant excavation and restoration of religious symbols and statues, new and old, accompany our endless searching to better known ourselves. To name and rename ourselves, to join, to leave and to convert. What are we turning away from? What are we converting? What are we turning toward as our humanity is taxed by disease, famine and war? My prayer is that we are turning to Love, with Love, and for Love.

As the global pandemic demands more inward, individual and collective soul-searching; I'm captivated by resilience and defiance, as emanating from a similar, and cohesive, consciousness and quest for morality. This constant searching, we do in the name of personal and interpersonal healing, answering ancient unchanging questions:

Who are we? Why are we here? Why do we suffer? Where do we go from here?

Electing to dissociate from the social order that religion creates, I now dive into the fear/fire, to burn away disillusionment. I have returned to the sweat lodge, and the peyote songs, of my initiation ceremony. I rely on Jesus, intellectually unashamed of that.

Choosing to lose myself, to the liberation surrender brings, not confining or defining myself according to this past or present, I vow to change by the minute.

It is how I understand, *Christ consciousness*, and why I cling to Jesus, and indigeneity that:

I experienced with direct and prolonged immersion in nature, alone, as a child, and through my four-day initiation ceremony, in the Lakota Sundance tradition, through sweat lodge and pipe ceremonies, with Cree spiritual leaders, elders and pipe carriers from Alberta and Edmonton Canada, at the age of 23. To me, and as John Trudell reminded us, in Hanging from the Cross, "Indians are Jesus hanging from the cross." I understand this, viscerally. I also know the spiritual turning from cerebral vascular accidents, especially the CVA I suffered in 1998. (My forthcoming book explores disability, medical intervention, harming and healing in depth.)

A note for historical orientation; I am watching, at this moment of editing, the Tribal Nations Leadership Summit at the Whitehouse with President Joe Biden, Vice President Kamala Harris, and Secretary of Interior Deb Halland.

I pray daily with my Spiritual advisor and mentor who is a Diné warrior, and American Indian Movement brother, and friend, from the Wounded Knee Occupation of 1973, Len Foster.

5

DISCLAIMER

Most of my poetry is an inner and outer exploration and inquiry. It is a process of uncovering, unveiling, imagining, and healing. It is deeply personal. I make no claims, or represent any of my biological siblings, or their experiences. My personal experiences, stories my mother shared with me, were my own, and hers, and ours. As the youngest of six children, I was mostly an only child, as they left home, some of them, far before I was ten years of age.

I experienced extreme bullying by some white kids, in Vienna, Virginia and Millis, Massachusetts in the 1970's and early eighties, who stereotyped me as Native, and who called me "nigger," leading my mother to share stories of ancestors who "transgressed," and married and produced children on her maternal and paternal side, with native people, who the white ancestors disowned.

Her marriage to my father, an African Egyptian Sudanese man, was "repeating the sin," to some, and accepted by others. This thread of love, that broke miscegenation laws and broke social and cultural mores, seems to be the love I draw upon for social justice and healing.

The period I spent living in Millis, Massachusetts, was a deeply troubled and trying time for me emotionally. My father who worked at the highest levels of the Department of Defense, was involved in an extra marital affair, negatively impacting my mother, and myself.

At the age of 13, I was sent for the summer to live with my brother and his wife, and then two-year-old daughter, who I babysat frequently, while they both worked. Again, at age 15, they legally adopted me, and became my guardians, sometimes to the exclusion of any contact with my parents for long periods of time.

During this time in which I was my oldest brother's legally adopted daughter, I was brutally attacked and raped on a bike path in a park behind their townhouse. The suppression of this horrific assault, caused me years of anguish, the pain of being misunderstood, and misrepresented by my siblings as emotionally difficult, unstable, and a "troublemaker."

The sudden and traumatic death of my horse, while I was in Virginia, and he was in Massachusetts, was the second devastating and psychologically destabilizing event that negatively impacted my soccer playing, and school performance.

Part of my radical disclosure of the traumatic events that punctuated a life marked with constant moving and upheaval is to show that one CAN heal and transform that which silenced and stunted us. It is only through prayer, and proper guidance with skilled healers and spiritual mentors, that I have been granted the chance to LIVE, and sometimes thrive, after domestic violence, rape, abuse, drugs, alcohol, violence, bullying, kidnapping, trafficking and ultimately rescue, renewal and redemption.

No sibling or association who claims to know me, can make any claims to the contrary of what has been or is true for me. We were born to the same parents, and we each had radically different lives, in different environments, in different states, with different rules. We are, estranged to one another. We were raised with different cultural and sociopolitical contexts.

We might as well have had different parents.

To the many friends, whose parents (in more stable or culturally mainstream, or loving homes) took me in as their own child, I thank you, for sanctuary and "normalcy," when things were too erratic for me to remain with my parents, who I loved beyond words, and who abandoned me in many instances, when their own lives were threatened, during a time when my mother protected the water, and during and throughout their long, adversarial divorce.

It is with complete love, forgiveness and gratitude that I write today. I love my parents and my siblings deeply, with reverence.

I write not as a victim or a martyr, I write to claim my future, one bathed in peace and protection, and the opportunity to write free of the toxic residue that trauma made. I am writing myself well, and whole, as a thriver rather than survivor.

The TRUTH is attractive to the soul, where the illusion is attractive to the Id, the, Ego. I listen for, bear witness to, and speak the truth, as a passport to liberation. I listen to "God."
My purpose and hope in candid disclosure is to help others, who may feel alone, and to illuminate the different emotional layers and texture of the healing journey.

My poetry is prayer,
my prayers are,
my protection.

A very special thanks to my spiritual advisor, AIM brother, friend, and
mentor, LF.

I choose to follow indigenous leadership. It the only way I
see, to protecting a future,
for seven generations to come.

Diné and Lakota, as I learn, as I pray...

Hózhó náhásdlíí. Hózhó náhásdlíí. Hózhó náhásdlíí. Hózhó náhásdlíí. Mitákuye Oyásin. Ahó.

In beauty it is finished, in beauty it is finished, in beauty it is finished, in beauty it is finished. All my relations, ahó.

Iowa

The land opened
before me,
A loving mother's hand
outstretched.

Gentle rolling hills,
a farm in the distance,
soft periwinkle light before dawn
warm yellow glows,
from the hearth.

Cow barn
bigger than the house,
Iowa.
Where my mother
was born.

Fire at four,
Ashes to ashes.
Her daddy left.
Divorce a scandal,
in the forties.
Neighbors speak in hushed tones,
Her only friends,
her dolls,
and younger brother.
Her mother went to work,
for the Southern Railway Company.

A Black woman came to raise them.
She loved her,
more than she loved her own mother.
Until she was sent to live with her grandfather,
in Baltimore,
beaten, beaten and beaten…
The strap, the belt, the brush.
Her comfort?

A bull, on a city side farm.
Never touched my Mom,
but chased boys to their near deaths!

"I could ride that bull!" she would boast...I believe her.
My brothers didn't graduate from high school,
they got Ph.D.'s in the World Cup Rodeo circuit.
They got that bull riding,
from my Momma.
Iowa,
Where my mother was born.

Egypt

He slept on a mud floor.
Siblings stolen,
by a hungry Nile.
Devouring swimmers and siblings.

Typhoid the thief.

Drowning future farmers.

My father from Egypt,
spared by lack of swimming ability,
carried his eight-year-old brother
to the doctor,
barefooted,
twenty-five miles to Alexandria.
Pronounced dead,
on arrival,
in his eleven-year-old arms.

My father from Egypt,
carried his brother
for the rest of his life.

Becoming a scientist,
attempting to save a whole world,
from invisible robbers,
and deadly wars.

Crossing to America,
standing
proud as pyramids,
before policemen and judges,
who bowed at the altars of prejudice and ignorance,
Not the Buddha of peace,
Jesus of Salvation,
human sanctity,
Not Ra, nor Isis,

not Mohammed the Prophet,
he left behind,
could stop the steady,
maniacal,
drip
drip
drip,
or
roaring falls,
of racism,
piercing his heart,
indelibly cruel
while he ignored it,
still;

it claimed his children.

A descendant of one of
the most ancient,
advanced civilizations,
in the world,
he arrived in Illinois,
was refused a marriage license,
to my mother
born in Iowa.

Exiled,
they returned to Egypt.
Nasser closed the doors to the West,
and now, they faced the same exclusion,
his village disapproving,
of their love,
those blended shades
of chocolate brown,
and ivory tusks.
They waited.
They watched,
and they were watched,
by Nasser's assassins,

until,
a dangerous escape,
to Libya,
from Libya,
to France,
from France,
to Canada,
back to America... where,
hate was more forgiving. In the sense that,
he would not as easily,
be killed,
for his sins of passion,
for my mother,
a blue-eyed American.

Speeding his way into whiteness,
trading peace
for fame and fortune,
trading prayers
for power,

offering

brilliance for brokerage,
my father from Egypt,
gathered his horses,
and fought
for our freedom.

In Nineteen Sixty-Eight,
he left for Viet Nam.
Returning more violent,
more unpredictable,
a stranger to my mom.

Battles won, and wars lost,
soul contracts broken.
Scorned by Mohammed,
the Imam called...

14

Nobody answers the calls to prayer anymore.

Egypt.
My myth,
and Mother.
My Africa.
My Nubia.
My Fatherland,
my dual citizenship,
un-enjoyed,
encumbered by fanatical religious
right winged conflagrations
political grudges,
lists are maintained.

Dust and dirt delivered my father,
to the white house,
where generals ordered,
where he served
and was served,
by Presidents,
Kings and Princes.

My Father from Egypt,
who, as a boy,
living in a British
occupied village,
in the twenties,
returned a soccer ball,
throwing it as a gesture,
(An omen to his future,)
kicked over a barbed wire fence,
by the British soldiers,
they carried him,
through the village,
cast a hero,
on the shoulders
of his occupiers.

15

My Father from Egypt,
who, along with Anwar Sadat,
wore shoes too big,
to attend the British school,
poor sons of a Tailor,
and a farmer,
taunted by the oppressors,
he vowed to rise like the Sun,
in the West,
recovering
lost brothers and sisters,
from the Nile,
who drank them.

Later...

Purifying waters,
walking down a rural road,
along the Charles River,
in Massachusetts,
he collected garbage,
from litterers,
and profiteers of
filth,
arrogance,
and consumption.

*He atoned for missing prayer
running before dawn.*

Gathering love,
and flowers,
adorning his neck,
a crown for my mother:
refusing to wear gold,

stolen from his homeland.

He gave me Egypt,

in a veil,
dripping with turquoise teardrops,
in boxes,
decorated with Kings and Queens,
Gods and Goddesses,
a shirt with Nefertiti,

*(the school called home to tell my mother I was wearing
an inappropriate shirt for picture day, and Nefertiti, lay
hidden behind a pink sweater, accompanied by my frown.)*

He gave me Egypt,
in Scotch whiskey,
in King Tutankhamen's head.
Poison in exchange for sorrow.

He gave me Egypt,
in tears of grief-stricken madness
at the loss of his entire family.
He gave me Egypt
in a box of coins,
to spend when I arrive there,
in the future that never comes...

Like sand falling
from open palms,
and open hearts,
turned upward toward heaven,
too late to return home...

My father of Egypt,
one of two survivors
of sixteen children,
cousins too many to count,
who I may never meet...

A sea,
a mirage,
beyond a horizon,

a desert,
an illusion,
collusion,
in front of the pyramids of Giza,
my father stands,
for the last time,
offering a rose to the psychic.

Covering my eyes,
I see my father from Egypt.
In the mirror,
he's looking back at me.

(In A Context of) Colonization

We gave them
Shelter
They gave us guns
We gave them food
They gave us alcohol

We gave them love
They gave us hate
We gave them trust
They gave us betrayal

They stole our land
We shared the rivers
They put up dams
We put down blankets

We gave them Mother Earth
They gave us churches

We gave them horses
They gave us cars
We gave them great Chiefs
They gave us politicians
We gave them spiritual leaders
They gave us priests

We gave them
Hesapa
They gave us
Washington DC

We gave them the lodge
They gave us government housing

We gave them Bear Butte
They gave us the Vatican
We gave them the open sky

They gave us prisons

We gave them shells
They called it money
We gave them fishing
They gave us Govt cheese

We gave them 500 nations
They gave us a country
We gave them "democracy"
They gave us oligarchy

We gave them another chance
They gave us spies and lies
We gave them our hearts
They gave us entrails

We gave them the good red road
They gave us highways

We gave them the pipe
They gave us communion
We gave them the Buffalo
They gave us Dominoes

We gave them herbs
They gave us diabetes

We gave them the sacred fire
They gave us air conditioning

We gave them thunder beings
They gave us white Jesus

We gave them hope
They gave us despair
We gave them air
They gave us pollution
They gave us problems

We have the solution

They gave us all colonization
We offer decolonization

Forked Tongues

They like our food,
but not our names.

Loose Horses

For my father

My horses were set loose one day,
My father lay ripped open
bleeding on the ground.

I heard the call for an ambulance on
the police scanner
in my friend's kitchen.

We had just finished eating
cookie dough
from a coffee can.

Mrs. Haggerty was a sure and steady Mom.
Now she just looked scared.
Her face contorted,
she hugged me.

Let's go,
your mother called.
She needs you home now,
your horses are loose.

Those horses I loved,

were sometimes dangerous.
They ponies kicked,
bucked and bit.

This time,
one of them
ran my dad under a pine bough,
sliced open his skull and shin.

He came home wrapped in gauze,
needing bourbon and rest.

They came and took that pony away.
I didn't care.

I was ten,
I was numb.
I only loved,
my horse.

Part two: nightmares

I dreamt of loose horses,
one named impatience,
one named fear,
one named ego,
the last one,
named desire.

Unbridled,
I ran after all four!

Like chasing bubbles that:
disappear,
or pop in your hands.
They consumed me.

Desperate,
Exhausted,

I flew over the accident scene,
a field of red poppies,
exploded,
beneath me,
I collapsed in the warm Sun,
I dreamed of my horses,
loose,
galloping,
bucking wildly,
I woke up from the dreams:
I struggled
to control my horses,
I forgot what I was chasing,
I forgot what I feared.
I looked out into the field,
Into the dream,
within the dream,
Four horses
Grazing quietly,
moving as One.

I walked away from the horses,
and I put down my gun.

Published online: May 25, 2013

Free

Winter skies,
skeleton trees,
death of lies,
lakes still freeze,
hibernation,
COVID days,
my liberation,
from your toxic gaze.

I Am the Mud

I am the mud,
on the bottom of the river Nile,
I am the mud,
on the bottom of the river Jordan,
I am the mud
on the bottom
of opposing shores.

Between a white shore,
and a Black shore,
is a river of mud…
I am the mud.

I am the mud,
in between,
I am the mud,
the unseen,
I am the mud,
on the bottom of the river…
I am the mud that:
churns up,
and disturbs
clearwater,
clear thinking…

I am the mud,
the ambiguity that swallows your feet,
when you try to walk in it…

I am the mud
in-between opposing shores…
and,
closed doors…

Between white and Black
is a murky undercurrent…
an unsteady step,

a confusing maze,
a light brown muddy haze…
I am the mud.

I am the mud
that is obscene!
I am the mud that comes up like:
water rushes…
and crashes…
through barriers and sandbags
of hatred and ignorance,
I am the mud that love made,
blurring the lines between shores.

I am the mud you don't want to step in,
or swim in,
I am the mud…
on the bottom of a river
called
LOVE!
that joins us
from opposing shores.

Children never fear the mud…

I am the mud.
I am the color red,
The red clay earth woman,
The color of mud.
my heart,
the lotus…

Caramel Colored Karma

Who am I?
I am mixed.
I am my people.
My people are Black.
My People are Brown.
My people are Red.
My people are high Yellow.
My people can pass for White.
My people are White.
My people cry tears,

THAT
Dry up
crystalize
and turn to salt
in the wounds
WHILE
we realize
the Sweetness
of our collective soul
Is like:
sugar that spilled
on the tables
of our ancestors
oppressors
WHO
carelessly wiped the spilled sugar away
into the trash
WHILE
blood spilled at the end
of the whip
THAT
cracked in your barn
WHILE
you pulled on the yarn
at the end of your needles
that turned and twisted

KNOTS
into a scarf of shame that strangled us
and you spoke
with your sharp
and cutting tongues
LIKE
the blade that cuts the voice
out of the throat
of the young
light brown mulatto
high yellow
almost White
one drop too dark
girl
you invited
INTO
your mansion of pain
I am my people
WE
are the refrain.
We are healing rain.
We are:

Caramel Colored Karma.

I Am Transcultural

For Sonia Nieto

Not to be mistaken for multicultural
transcultural,
As in:
transcending,
transforming
transitioning
transient
transcultural being.

Slicing through borders and boundaries,
like icing splits middle ground.
Cakewalk.

I am here,
and there,
simultaneously.

I am my ancestors,
in Egypt,
and in Sudan,
I am them.

I am my ancestors in Scotland.
I am my ancestors in Ireland,
escaping persecution.
I am the French Huguenots in Quebec.
I am the Abenaki warrior.
I am the undocumented Métis.
I am the initiated Cree,
The lost and found in Lakota lands,
and Blackfoot intermarried,
undocumented, unwanted, mixed breeds,
"The last baby born in Fort Wayne, Indiana."
who bleed the same blue blood,
that turns red,
when we awaken.

I am the Pharaoh.
I am the Nubian Queen.
I am the white bred
middle class neoliberal.
I am the Black ghetto
Goddess.
I am the welfare mother.

I am transcultural.

I am you,
and you are me,
and I am we.
Transculturally transfixed.

I listen to God.

I am fluid like a river that blends opposing shores.
I am timeless.
I am transcultural.

Qu'aranic *Shift* In Five Verses

My father
brought a Koranic shift,
to my mother's apple pie.

I was too young
to notice
my Black Daddy. It was still okay
to sit on his lap
watching
Muhammad Ali fight.

I was too young
to notice
my Black Daddy
teaching me Arabic,
reciting the Koran.

I was too young
to notice,
all the White people,
in our house,
or that my mother
was forgetting
how to speak Arabic.

I was seven
when I started to notice,
my Daddy,
Black.
I stopped sitting on his lap,
hid
in stores,
with glaring,
staring,
White people.
(better to go out to the stores with Mommy.)
even if

they do ask,
if I'm adopted.

Even if she did,
tell him to stop,
eating with his hands,
smacking his stuffed cheeks,
burping with delight.
Even if she did,
tell him to stop,
"making that GAWDAWFUL NOISE!"
While he contemplated
his home,
where his noise,
was complimentary.

"That entire country stinks!"

she was angry.

Love doesn't plan
for racism.

I noticed,
my daddy Black.
Along with everybody else.

Verse Two:
They noticed me,
right away,
on the blacktop,
1st Day,
new school,
blonde-blue-eyed-Barbie-girls,
blood and salt,
dripping down,
my freshly stabbed face,
Embedded lead.

"Teacher!" I cried,
she sent me
back
to the "discipline desk."
Facing the wall.
Sentenced to sit
next to the kid
who stabbed me.

She screamed at me.
"Don't you ever interrupt my reading group again!"
They noticed me.

"You're ugly brown!"
they taunted.
"What are you a dirty little Indian?"

They formed a jeering circle.

Blurry chanting: through tears…
"OOOO WOOO WOOO WOOO! OOO WOO WOO WOO!"
cupping their cruel faces…

8th GRADE GRADUATION…
"Look there's a nigger here!"
They noticed my Black Dad,
"Sand Nigger!"
"Jiggaboo!"
"Nigger Nips!"
"National Geographic Special!"
"Gypsy Girl!"
"NIGGER!"

I noticed how much…
I
hated him. like,
they hated me.
like,
I hated them,

how,
I hated me...

Verse Three

Eight years later,
another new school.

"Yellow Bitch!"
"White Bitch!"
"Mixed Nut! Half Breed! Oreo!"
"Spanish Girl!"
The girls said,
the Black girls said,

"Egyptian Princess!"
"Black Queen!" *"Goddess!"*
"Honey-Comb!"
"Café Au Lait!"
"Nefertiti!"
"Cléopâtre!"

The boys said,
the Black boys said.
I started to notice,
my Black roots,
my Black Daddy,
working so hard,
to be White,
just like me,

wishing and praying,
my hair blonde,
my eyes blue.

Oh, I noticed,
how they lied,
in school,
lied at home,
lied on T.V.

I noticed truth

37

shimmering
on the surface
thousands of diamonds
coming to me
and this time
I didn't let them
steal them.

Verse Four
Part Two
"Sheriff John Brown"

My white-wanna-be,
badge-wearing
terrifying
sheriffying
brother.
my hero,
noticed me.
He was the first,
to notice me,
getting Black.

*"If you bring one home,
I'll kill 'em!"*

He noticed...
He threatened,
"I'll shoot to kill!"
They noticed me,
Right out of the family.

Verse Five:
headlines

After eighteen years
A blonde blue-eyed-wanna-be
was found in Washington D.C.
at the Roxy
with some Rastafarians.
She was out of place,
(but never taunted.)

The Egyptian girl
American born
raised in the States
among privileged white folks
was reclaimed today
by her African sisters and brothers
where she was brought
into
the loving branches
of her
true family tree,
Black inclusion
infusion
a tincture
at last.

Verse Five:
Update

After spending years,
in the university
mis-educated by false prophets
worshiping false idols
a woman passed out
in a class

after learning
she had been whitened
to an almost
unrecognizable state.

Fortunately,
her black soul
saved her life.

She awakened
painfully
like a captured mustang
she learned
That getting too Black
in classes
and meetings
is dangerous.

White people see her as ethnic.
Egyptians feel pity for her,
because she was
"Americanized"
fooled by their own delusion
that somehow
they aren't?

Some Black people
see her as White
Indian
Latinx
She sees herself as
Love
Energy
Light
Indigenous.
to Earth.

She is just trying to live
certain

41

of her Blacknicity,
her indigeneity,
Praise the Lord,
Black Jesus.

A Simple Plan to Eradicate Racism

Multiracial people,
have a story.
It's not *half* the story.
It's not a *quarter* of a story.
It's not a *uniform* story.
It's not quantifiable,
or measured in percentages for
tribal rolls.

It is a holy
human,
whole story.

It a medicine story.

It's a love story.

The census needs two categories
on the way to no categories:
for political purposes

Black and White.

For decolonization,
through unification,
of African,
Asian,
and Indigenous.

The same way
European
Caucasian
groups

became White.

Then we need to dismantle that shit
once and for all.

The Table of Chocolate Secrets

I can remember,
the table where,
my mother
held council,
with her friends.

The table where,
thousands of words,
smelled like coffee,
and chocolate.

Across the table,
salty tears,
were exchanged,
left lingering in the air,
for me to breathe.

The table where crimes,
of their husbands,
were revealed.
The husbands,
who paid for
the boxes
they kept their lives
locked in.

I was flung across that table,
a ragdoll flying,
from the hands of my mother's husband,
in a fit of rage.

The conversations,
at the table of chocolate secrets,
fascinated me,
while the wood,
and its displaced rings,
held my steady gaze.

tracing lines on a table,
that could not hold,
the weight of the lies,
and fights,
that surfaced there.

I listened to our neighbor,
crying about her daughter,
who tried to kill herself,
again,
and her mother again.

Julia,
who loved,
and feared,
in the fields,
where she screamed,
naked at night,
until,
sirens,
blared,
and flashed red,
across my walls,
making my heart race,
to the tempo,
of her agony.

The sirens,
the knife,
she tried to stab her mother with,
in the kitchen,
of their pink and perfect house,

would be relived,
the next day,
over chocolate and coffee,
served on the surface,
of the table.

Sometimes,
they would offer me,
an anger-coated,
sorrow-soaked,
chocolate,
and talk,
as if I wasn't there.
hearing how they,
strapped up Julia,
again,

in a straight jacket,
and took her away,
again,

and how she fought,
and they injected her,
and they held her down.

I wondered,
if my mother knew,
that it was Julia,
who kept me,
squeezing me
tightly,
covering my mouth,
telling me to be quiet,
under the Forsythia bushes,

Telling me,
"you shouldn't trust her!"
my mother,
while she screamed frantically for me,
from the top of the garage,

while I couldn't breathe,
and couldn't move,
Julia held me so strongly,
under the sea of yellow,

and tangled branches.

She promised me,
that she would "feed me dinner,"
there,
under the Forsythia,
where my mother,
wouldn't find me,
and take me away from her,
and kill me.

There,
at the table of chocolate secrets,
my mother and her best friend,
choked on the stories
that fabricated their lives,
with their
"sons-of bitches-no-good husbands!"
who,
they murdered,
over and over again,
at the table of chocolate secrets.

After The Fire

The jaws of the
monstrous,
lifeless,
house,
black jagged teeth,
stalactites
of death,
crystalized soot,
charred memories,
and remains,
of the flames,
that
licked the sky,
sending smoke,
and burnt offerings,
to an unworshipped God,
leaving them alive,
to walk through the ruins,
feeling dead.

The melted Ming,
like broken wings
of a dead crow,
table legs strewn,
like smoldering logs,
scattered,
frosted days,
encase,
smothered lives,
each step,
a walk-through hell,
black teeth descending,
from beams.

The throat of the house.

cursing members,

49

of the family cast,
emerging
from dark and icy depths,
"from the belly of the beast."
Piano pile.

A family opera
in the key of ash.
Dreams turned to dust.
A black spot
on a white blanket,
deeply piled snow,
pillows of sorrow,
no traces of life.
Sliding along the black tongue,
with effort
and attention,
I greet and hug,
my molester,
in the gut
of the slayed dragon.

Dancing For Tears

I sit and wait
for tears
they come at their discretion
when guards relinquish
their steady post
at the gate to my heart.

I pray for tears
like my ancestors.
Rain-dancing.
Drumming on the desert
of my subconscious.

Mirages of winged angels
drape clouds
over the iniquitous valley
that hides children,
locked in
closets,
by heavy hands
and delinquent deliverers.

The iniquitous valley,
where oceans absorbed
sobbing skies
who bled
for the rivers
of her mother.

I am waiting
for dawn to
break a silence
that hurt my ears,
with sirens
warning
of loneliness,
and confusion.

Madness made
of innocence lost.

During interrupted dreams
terrorist attacks.
In the beds of sleeping angels,
fallen fathers
prey upon their own young.
Yearning tender caresses
of youth's friendships,
Summer's
that held me whole
in forever,
before suited men
stole every bit of aging flesh,
from a body
already ravaged by vultures.

Vultures
who smell death
and weakness
in the souls
of tortured
dismembered
bodies
of unwanted
and abandoned
children.

Born into desolate wealth
impoverished castles,
built on lies
and secrets
generals share,
while they booze
and travel,
bringing back
lifeless dolls
to the living dead.

I wait
for tears
to quench arid thirsty plains
and flatlands
of my body,
that stretches
and snaps
seeking pain
a soul's reminder,
a spirit
still exists
un-extinguished,
in the cloudless
thunder less
night.

Summer Souls

The hills and valleys
of his form,
bronze,
iron and timeless,
invite me in-
holding me-
like a winding river,
to his oceanic soul,
where I am tossed,
and caressed,
like a sailboat,
in a gentle wind,
on the sea,
before a storm.

Bird song
For my mother, Elizabeth Searle
b. 1930 d. 1996

First sounds of worship,
feathered flyers,
brush wings
against the sky,

brush strokes

painting the Sun,
dawn comes,
we took her for granted,

someone didn't wake up today.

My portal here,
gone.
Mother ship,
gone.

Lost my way home,
too young,
to know the difference,
between a mother -figure,
or an evil witch,

She painted birds for a living.

Vultures came,
after the ceremony,
asking:

*"please could I have just one,
to remember her…"*

until I had nothing left
to give

an amber necklace,
an antique quilt,
drunk,
I had no path,
a pin,
a painting,
a vase,
to erase her
from my memory.

I make offerings,
at the temples,
twelve years,

negotiating a sign,

while a lawyer wants
records of the car accident
at nine,
that sent me into glass,
too strong
to kick out,
and escape
drowning.

First sounds of worship,
feathered flyers,

brush strokes against the sky,

painting the moon
dusk comes,
telling the setting Sun,
we took her for granted,

someone didn't wake up today.

I rise on thermals,
closer to crows and hawks,

than humans.
Comfort in the cardinal,
alms to sparrows,
who sing me a tomorrow,
she took with her
when she left.

Trinkets her treasures,
spread across the world.
Scattered like
bones I found
in her ashes,
unexpectedly,
unknown,
she comes in the morning,
And says,
"Shhhhhhhhh…"

It's all right,
I'm your birdsong now.
"You can't fly
carrying around pianos,
paintings,
and necklaces
now,
can you?"

"Shhhhhh…Shhhhhhh…. Shhhhhh…."
She is the wind….

Birdsong,
first sounds of worship,
feathered flyers,
brush wings
against the sky,
brush strokes,
she paints me an angel,
and horses,
with cloud paint,

and
I soar with her.

Hit'Em Hard

Resplendent porphyry.
The porous heart.
Innermost crystal.
Exposed now,
and vulnerable,
to onlookers '
contempt.

For shine
and refracted light,
set loose
after a million years,
of locked up brilliance.
Sealed during the mother's rage.
Fiery liquid drowning.
Rainbow light,
shining,
on the flying pigskin,

Ball of sorrow,
delivering hands,
trembling in the air,
of uncertainty.

Vulnerable souls,
being taught to be men.
A phalanx
in the autumn field.
All aglow,
in sun's setting,
on nostalgia's promise.
In the youthful parade,
of machismo's ghosts.

My son,
on the line,
just to the right of center,

guarding hope,
as he learns,
to
"HIT 'EM HARD!"
Only igneous rock is left,
on the field.

Crystal innocence,
shimmers away.
Forgotten.

At nine years old,
at 6:45 pm.
Like a shattered coke bottle,
cast in the asphalt of time.
Stolen,
by unsung heroes,
looking,
for a second chance,
at glory.

Listen Here Bullies

I am a ferocious wolf
dressed up in sheep's clothing,
to put meat on the table for my son.

My pain runs deep,
like a river
that collected
years of tears
from my brothers and sisters,
who cried
from the insults you slung.
Like mud in my face,
while I was only trying to play.

You surrounded me at recess
like blonde Barbie dolls.
Daughters of the soldiers
for the colonial agenda.

To shred my dignity.

I pace like an angry tiger,
at the zoo.
Waiting to maul my keepers,
with words
that will set me free,
from the white lies,
that are set in my mind,
like iron bars,
in concrete,

You tried to imprison my identity.

You called me:
"Nigger, jigaboo, ugly African, Pocahontas"
and you laughed heartily,
walking back and forth,

singing in my face,

"walk like an Egyptian..."

How does it feel?
To see Columbus decapitated?
Thrown in a river!
Now, that colonialism is dead?
Along with your ancestors,
who tried to annihilate us,
and silence our songs.

I wait for the chance
to reveal myself to you.
The object of your hatred,
the target of the guns,
your tongues,
the bullets:

Words...

I turn those words back to you,
and say:

"Shut the FUCK UP!"

Because it is our turn to talk!
I take off my sheepskin jacket,
Take a seat at your table,
and say.

"Grace."

Goose Down Memory of Friendship

For Charlotte

A soft voice woke me,
"C'mon, get up"
She whispered, insistently.
My resistant thoughts:

Why climb from a downy nest?
A pillow in heaven?
And sweet feathery dreams?

Yielding,
we tiptoe,
not to wake her parents.

Taking our first chilly steps,
to the bathroom,
where tiles are set,
like a chessboard,

In Black and White games,
White, always goes first.

Our stage floor,
of childhood's longest tubs,
wishes are bubbles.

Sliding on our jeans,
winding our way,
through the cold house,
we stop and stoke the wood stove,
in the heart
of the house.

Out the glass paned door,
into winter's clean breath...
greeted by muted neighs,
and nickers,

Steam rising,
billowing
from soft noses,
of hungry horses...
like clouds that form,
from ocean storms...

(we would come to pass through our own)

saddled up,
we rode into dawn,
steam rising-
Each hoof,
striking the ground,
like a skilled artisan,

hammering out
an enduring design,
on snowy trails,
glistening....
with promises
we take with us,
into the sanctuary of time,
an enduring gift,
only the two of us,
can open,
in adulthood.

Karma drew its circle,
around the hearts
of two friends...
silently,
Junipers,
accepted
strong
overlooking boughs,
of protective Pines,
overhead,
branches

outstretched
reaching for the Sun.
Speaking movement,
no words-
these friends,
found one another,
in the wind.
Galloping through ages,
nothing lost,
lessons from the longest days,
giving them a glimpse
of love,
and sweet reprieves,
during life,
and her cruel tests.

Cancer at Night

Liquid suffering,
Dilaudid delusions,
pain grips-
bones snap.

Tumors grow,
cancer steals her flesh.
I listen,
she whispers,
through fevers,
and chills,
on frosted nights…

I wait for her
to call me
to her bedside.
Impending death,
promises:
truth and laughter,
sweat and tears,
shit and blood,
love and sorrow.
Her body decays:
at the discretion,
of cells,
gone awry.

Her soul
drifts on-
the peace
of tomorrow.

Morning
delivers us-
from fear's
companion-the dark,
lonely minutes,

lasting for eternity…
Exhale…
a spirit sets sail.

Autumn

Trees wear leaves,
like tattered gold necklaces,
Clinging
to a weakened clasp.

Roots get trampled,
staying strong,
when getting walked on,
by the leisure class,
is all they know.

The sun plays hide and seek,
like a playful child,
Clouds hang heavy,
pregnant with rain.

Streams reflect,
light and color,
like a newly polished mirror,
while crows gather,
in crew cut corn fields.

Dressed for the funeral
all in Black.
Cacophonous cawing,
warning of the silent hawk.

Who suddenly descends,
like an arrow,
shot from heaven,
piercing Earth,
turning the unsuspecting,
hare into dinner.

Confident
of the day's success,
hunters retreat early.

Surrendering day to dusk,
the hesitant opal moon,
rises slowly,
illuminating the forest,
like a warm orange nightlight.
A cinnamon Earth,
the stage,
where winds howl,
like a chorus.

Trees sway,
like hungry skeletons,
dancing for a sleeping audience.

Awakening is slow,
like Autumn,
holding the fruits
of summer's laborers,
like pirates,
with their overflowing chests,
of treasures.

Bejeweled and bewildered,
we all gather
and release

uncertainty…

Preparing for a cold death.

A surrender,
that only detachment,
can bring,
or an unhinging,
like pawning
the last ring,
from an abandoning parent.

Falling,

like leaves,
in a crisp hymn,
final gestures,
become seeds.

Blowing from the palms,
seeds like ancestors,
Milkweeds: carelessly drift,
whispering,
of an eternal Spring.

The Lake

Dreaming:
my mind,
the Sun.

Thoughts,
clouds.

Water,
corpus.

Waves,
voice.
Singing ancient Earth songs,
lapping a mantra.

While you sleep.

Dragonflies like a melody.
Butterflies a ballet.
My arms,
the stage.

Diamonds of sparkling light,
tattoo my skin.

The surface:
an imperceptible membrane,
separating worlds.

One where:
gravity rules.
A heavy heart,
sinks like a stone.
The other:
liquid.
weightless,
a mind floats.

Breath in measures:
bubbles,
like blown glass.

A serendipitous sea,
collects
lost
and found souls,
like spare change.

I kayak the narrow opening,
threading the water,
and light.

I am the needle:
passing through the opening,
fresh water,
churning salty.

Leaving the lake,
turning toward the wild,
leaving the elegant shore.

safe harbor:
the tether to my soul.

Bradley at the Days Inn

Bradley was a frail young man,
tattooed by God,
he didn't carry a cross.
It carried him.

Sanity slipped,
from his sister Cheryl Ann,
in a motel room.
by highway 49.

The needle didn't deliver,
and powdered pills lay strewn,
across the floor.

Like stars from a heaven,
they fell from,
Earthbound,
they fell,
shooting away
forgotten dreams.

The Man Named *Rouen*

Dedicated to all casualties of the Viet Nam War.
This poem is a true story.

The man,
named
Rouen,
emerges from his car,
with a limp,
in a clear plastic poncho,
covering,
the orange Asplundh sweatshirt,

(Made in Viet Nam)

Khaki cargo shorts,
just below the knee,
white socks,
worn worked in Timberlands,
he limps,
thinking it strange,
he need not take cover,
this rain is as clean as his soul,
that escaped,
refugee work camps,
in Thailand.

The land beneath his feet,
clear of mines,
like the one,
that ate his whole family,
after his mother,
turned to yell at him to:

"Hurry up!"

just as he raised his head,
and glanced away,
from the ant pile,

that distracted him,
and caused the distance to grow,
and his hand to slip,
suddenly,
from his mother's grip.

The mine went off:
Sending his mother,
his father,
his grandmother,
his two older brothers,
and his little sister,
shooting into the air,
like an exploding star.

The suitcase,
containing the family's,
entire belongings,
hit him in the leg,
knocking him unconscious.

When he woke up,
he found himself,
in the jungle,
where he followed,
the others,
alone,
through Viet Nam,
all the way to America.

He thought he would never hear the word
WAR
again.
Now he relives the nightmare
over and over again…
while the wars rage on…

He comes out of the elementary school,
leading his granddaughter,

by her wrist,
so that he never has to feel,
a loved one's hand,
slipping away,
and letting go,
again.

My Feet Are a Map
"Dedicated to Janet Aalfs"

I thought I left grief behind this morning,
and met her in my feet.

They stuck to the floor.

My feet are breathing,
for my lungs,
that can't.

I dove in the ocean,
decided,
to meet,

Fear.
Face to face.

Deep underwater,
in silence.
Angelfish,
watched me drown.
While grief sliced
the water,

like a Barracuda,

I looked at its teeth.
like stalactites,
and stalagmites.

My feet are fins,
gracefully,
swimming,
fast.

I'm in the forest.

77

My feet won't let go,
of the shadow,
that walks in front of me.

Befriending
the dark,
I close my eyes.
So I can see better.
Instruments sit silently,
on a stage,
waiting to sing.

Musical notes
are starlings.
That fly
off the page,
and greet,
the hearing.

On strings,
pulled,
caressed,
and sprung.

I'm awake,
in this space,
where we meet as one.
Please don't look at me,
to know me,
look at my paintings,
my photographs,
my poetry,
to find,
feet that do not fit,
in European sized shoes,
properly.

Find my feet,
burned,

in deserts of desires.

Blistered on walks,
going nowhere,

broke

fighting losing battles,
feet that fell in love,
with sand,
and mud.

I have forgotten to thank my feet,
that I put in my mouth,
when I insulted you,
and fell.

My feet slipped,
on the edge of a Jacuzzi.
Stealing my arms,
head splitting on concrete,
face first,
making planning hard,
to do with a bruised,
pre-frontal cortex.

My feet are a map,
remembering shards of glass,
piercing them at sunrise,
outside of the county jail,
they walked me to freedom.

Feet fail.
Feet save.
Feet lie.
Feet lead.
Following my feet
leads me to a room
in "the memory palace,"

I am rubbing her feet,
we are 12.
We are friends,
Nantucket joy,
interrupted by her father,

screaming,
he runs toward her,
he slaps her face,
he pulls me off the couch,
by my feet.

And says,
"You're not doing
that 'lezbo footsie'
shit under my roof!"

It became dangerous to trust my feet.

Return of the Bamyan Buddha

"For Sister Clare Carter"

When they took the Buddha at Bamyan,
prophets knew,
it would come to this:
dancing around the same fire,
arguing about how hot the flame is,
marauding money launderers,
stalking the hearts of the innocents,
building their castles,
with bricks,
made from cow dung,
stolen from poor farmers' mounds.

Crows heckling hawks,
hawks, soaring and surveying,
the damage,
while profiteers' prostitute,
at the altars of fallen angels,
babies wilt at the tits of
Earth mothers,
and thugs jail
water protectors,
young soldiers dot the hillsides,
fatigued by dust,
and dismantled dreams,
like ants they march,
for a false King.

Seen by the Buddha
like a steady snake
sliding up the hillside,
to Bamyan.
Silk dresses,
carried in a burlap coffee sack,
hidden treasures,
to seduce their tongues later,
after destroying a thousand-year-old symbol of hope,

for the faithful,
silk gathered along the road,
to arouse temptations,
and a soft touch,
that delivers a heavy blow.

PART TWO

What drives this caravan of hands?
Hands that steal and slash the handiwork of healers?

Who turned the wheel in minds of men?
Who become,
a phalanx,
of dimly lit faces,
leathered by a forgotten future,
and a scorching sun.

Their smoking guns,
hot with greed,
the hillside,
dotted with grief,
meditating monks,
humming like a hive,

all the people who were told,
and sold,
to give up something,
to become something else.
Writing desperate pleas to their ancestors,
looking for evidence they existed before.
Before the noxious noise of machines,
before the tyranny of technology,
that gave them membership,
into the devil's country club.

Searching their bloodlines and DNA,
as if looking for lost keys,
arriving at the same places.
Places left,
where ghosts have faces,
traces.

Boats adorn the edge of primordial rivers.
Winding wide,

like pregnant women.
Asking for passage,
back to the Nile,
the Ganges,
the Kabul,
the Thames,

to find out what went wrong,
to find nothing,
and everything.

On a pilgrimage to Bamyan.
Where Buddha towers above the carnage and corpses.
Where Mohammed sings again in Mosul,
and Jesus walks on water in Venice.
Where lions sleep with lambs,
and we make ourselves
Kintsukori
bodies as offerings.
And dig up the severed hands,

"The hands that make the mudra have no fear."

Ferrying willing passengers,
to Bamyan.
Where broken limbs,
become dust,
dust that settled on soldiers 'cups,
coating empty bowls,
like honey to a burn.

Dust become stars,
stars become planets,
the Lotus blooms forever,
and The Buddha at Bamyan
returns.

Ode to Lives Lost In 2016

Echo...
Echo...
Echo...
chamber,
open and loaded,
safety is off,

Echo...
Echo...
Echo...
"Black Lives Matter
as much as White Lives Matter?"
is just an illusion,
cuz' its cops killing our Black sons,
who are natives to this land,
take my hand,
while I lead you to the menu,
of our great nation's history,
what about,

Herstory?

The one where she was raped,
while they walked,
through the white only turnstile,
and smiled at Langston Hughes,

"Strange fruit"

and brute force,
that stole the breath,
out of the last captives,
while they left them,
to become radioactive,
and all they asked was:

"does he find her attractive?"

as they walked down
Hollywood Boulevard,
completely unaware,
of the dead woman,
lying behind,
the white picket fence,
in the neighbor's yard,
she was trying to run,
but he fired the gun...

they kept walking

and around the corner,
was little Jack Horner,
spray painting graffiti,
of the resurrected Nefertiti,
while they walked on by,
singing:

"Walk like an Egyptian."

900 Count Egyptian cotton,
picked in the USA,
200 years,
ago,
while the Latina Quincinerra,
was being called a "hoe!"
while her daughter remarked,

"but Mami,
I thought slavery ended though?"
you know,
the way little kids say,
"though?"
at the end of a sentence,
when they reveal the truth,
like a line from Ruth,
but the teacher is lying,
to keep her third job?

Doe a deer,
a female deer,
we think it queer,
what we unlearn in a year,
steering the Tesla,
to the gravedigger's ear.

Graçias A La María Hynes Y Bobi Céspedes

Aprendiendo
prayers,
Cuban música.

Entiendo más que puedo hablar,

Entonces,
es necesario
empezar
incluso si
Tú tienes temor.
Escrito en español,
un otro idioma,
del colonizador.

Anoche,
el Título de la canción,
que Bobi Escribió,
sobre su Madre

"Anoché."

I imagine,
my apartment building
has no walls,
I buy my subscription,
to the San Francisco Jazz,
on Friday nights,
para cinco dólares,
I add a twenty-five-dollar donation,
para los artistas,
la música,
a través de,

entonces,
empiezo a bailar,
to dance,

A Bobi.

"Anoché,"

me imagino,
while I dance,
on an imaginary dance floor,
en una pista de baile imaginaria.

Recuerdo
mi introducción,
al Jazz.
A Miles Davis.
In a white Honda Prelude,
on 395 South,
the Capital Beltway,
he belts out Tutu,
we glide,
we ride,
to Richmond,
car full of musicians,
smoke and Jazz.

Tutu.
Recuerdo
es ahora,
es el futuro,
en este momento es tanto,
el presente pasado y futuro,

I imagine,
there is,
no pandemic.
What is the word
for Pandemic in Spanish?
Pandémico?

What is the word for beautiful in Congolese?
Nzuri.

Mrembo.
Colonizers were there also.
Mrembo became:
Belle Magnifique…

Bobi es,
Mrembo Nzuri,
in Congolese,
in west Africa,
in Cuba.

No more pillagers.
No more plagues.
Columbus es muerte!

"Anoche!"
Baile sin vergüenza.
Baile sin arrepentimiento.
Sin culpa.

Having made
earlier confessions,
with "Padre"
del Norte,

*God's cottage by the sea,
in Ireland.*

On You Tube.

In my mind,
my wings open,
to the sky.

Like Sly Stone,
in 1968,
*my mom "Betty,"
holds me for the first time.*

Betty, Mike and Sly
hook up,
to take us all higher,
I absorb the high vibrations,
and frequencies of love.

Threads of sound,
invisibly drawing us together,
across lines,
the colonizers drew,
all around us,
to keep us in,
to keep us out.

Love makes its way,
around barbed wire,
under and over fences,
and across enemy lines.
Then.
Now.
Tomorrow.

Mitakuyé Oyasín.
Mitakuyé Oyasín.
Mitakuyé Oyasín.

Blended people,
are Jazz.
Sound calls us,
like prayer.

Words the afterthought,
describing deep impressions,
first,
there was the sound.
And the sound was God.

AUM.

An infant's cry.
A 1952 chevy driving through
mud puddles in a field in Cuba.

WHOOSH!
We arrive and depart
in a sound.

Words drip,
from the end of the pen,
fast as flight,
Starlings clap,
leaving,

the last cornfield gleaned.

We arrive.
We speak.
We depart.

Jazz is never free.

Before Jazz is pain.

"Anoché."

There is no pandemic
in my apartment.

I'm watching live Jazz,
recorded months ago,
in San Francisco.
I tear down the walls,
and dance with my neighbors,
in a party.

"Anoche."

Escrito en español

sin temor.

Los errores son oportunidades.

We dance!
We sing!
We laugh!

"Anoche."

Escrito en español.
Por qué
es necesario.
Empezar.

Return

For Peg and Andy

Burnt trees,
stand statuesque,
after Winter's cruel burn.

Icy fingers
lose their grip,
in Spring's refrain,
birds return.

Singing me
home.

Google: God's Thresher

God the reaper bearer,
wind winnowing souls.
Threshing out sinners,
harvesting His saints.

And what of our time?

Technology the tool,
or, technology,
the Grim Reaper.
The Internet:
Mechanization of God.
Thresher of Babylon

desires.

Like, incessant radioactive rain,
flooding rooms,
in places of the mind,
no more closed doors.
Secrets are out.
Drowning in temptations,
to buy and sell.
Human commodities.
Slavery flourishing in plain sight.
Ordinary becomes extraordinarily.
rare.
Celluloid celebrity souls.

You Tube!
Suddenly everyone is a star!
Selfies,
staring into an endless mirror,
reflecting,
the Macro Ego,
for consumption.
The great conflagration.

And the small remnant.
Dying or surviving in obscurity.
Waiting patiently.

Cyber footprints,
God's new
naughty or nice list.
It is easier for an elephant in the room,
to enter through the eye of the needle,
to type a text,
than it is for trolls
and lost souls,
of the matrix,
to enter the gates of Heaven.

Abandoners of truth,
justice and the sacred law.
Leaving the last harbinger of truth,

human sanctuary

the body temple,
where secrets and misdeeds,
could lay in wait,
for old age.
And judges at the seat of one's own soul,
now
no escape.
Google is God:
And the reckoning day comes,
Where judgment beats its gavel down,
with a final sentencing,
to ones with a wicked thirst,
to Own,
and scoff,
and play God,
In the playgrounds of fools,
How will we walk? Less upright,
after scoliosis sets in,

and we can no longer,
raise our heads up to pray.

Stardust

We are sand.
We glitter broken.
Scattered,
still alive,
we shine.

Reflecting losses:
our last lives,
on our shared and
webcast star.

We enter the water ceremony,
of our sorrowful mother.
Dreaming and drowning,
ourselves into
a greener world,
where we might find
love and laughter,
company for the way.

Trampled and heavy,
waves crash here,
tugging and tearing the shores,
like a toddler
pulls his mother's
shirt,
having been ignored,
on the verge of a tantrum.

Warm mud,
coats our faces,
we see Earth,
in the mirror,

like seeing our own faces,
for the first time,
after a harrowing accident

left us disfigured.

Interlocking roots,
our soul fibers,
true connection,
our networks,
trees.

Leaves always listen.

Tangled mycelium,
netting us here:
like a desperate fisherman,
holding the sphere,
afraid of losing humanity
his prized catch.

When we cry,
we taste
the salted past.

When we sleep,
we are space.

Eyelids wide,
like
dark drapes,
covering windows,
to new worlds:

we have only yet
to draw them open,
finding them,
already here,
within.

Thoughts are gone:
wind scrapes our ancestors loose.
Bones from boulders.

Our weary Grandmother's shoulders.

Wearing hand knitted shawls,
like decorated deserts,
waiting for camels
and soldiers,
to deliver news,
of all wars end.

Grieving here.
Stardust by the sea.
Once suspended:
timeless,
the heart,
our planet,
beating eternally,
becoming the sound
of the primordial river.

Carrying silt to oceans,
who hoard the rain,
we wear grief
like atmospheric
cloud cover,
storm clouds,
threaten thunder
and don't deliver.

Our veins,
narrowing,
until the volcanic embolism,
stops Earth's
incessant breathing.

The quiet killing virus
came to us,
so, our lying could stop.
Long enough for truth to rise,

like sea foam
and
bioluminescent Mar Eel.

Paradise shimmers:
she holds
us in Her dazzling light,
Every-time we
let go,
we renew Her.

Like dropped stitches,
and forgotten pearls,
humans drop off the edge of steel wings,
screaming after Afghanistan,
invasions
left sores and gaping wounds,
scarring her skin and skeins.

The Red Storm
kills the fishermen.
Sand buries the living.
Forests are scattered toothpicks,
sold for the last fires.

Coals and embers,
searing our minds
memory
is too long
for time.

We are all refugees.
Cutting our Achilles tendons
on the barb wired
fences we made
to keep
ourselves away
from ourselves.
Governments find fear easier

than a widening of the arms.
A family of eight in Madagascar,
cut up a sweet potato,
calling it dinner,
while a king
wines and dines,
in Saudi Arabia,
surveying cars,
in his private collection.
Borrowing a tired line
from the emperor,
who couldn't lend him a shirt.

Like flies on rotting flesh,
it's never enough,
for the greed infested,
maggot laden,
stomachs of the takers,
and over consumers,
drinking the blood of our mother,
oil their spoils,
and murderous wails,
children crying from underground jails,
with no tickets to freedom.

A young girl sits
in a sun-soaked forest,
smelling cedar and pine,
sleeping with the princesses.
She sees the Northern flicker,
she offers the rare bird
corn pollen,
she's walking barefoot,
hugging the sunbaked rocks,
smoothed out by glaciers.

She remembers herself awake.
The nightmare ends.
She places her hand,

in a cold rushing brook,
telling Her she is,
a water protector.
She re-members us,
a future,
and calls us home.

The Funeral of Betty Wild

Strings pulled
taught,
across empty honey pots,
clinging notes,
slip toward heaven.

Fallen angels,
fill wings,
of hospitals,
turned morgue.

The walking dead
look like bandits.
Nowhere left to rob,
everything is online,
Presto
Crypto

sends thieves
who litter the skies
with private jets.

Yachts like spilled pearls
too big for small seas,
dolphins line beaches
like tombstones.

No more unexpected whispers,
between strangers:
People fill out applications,
to meet someone,
Just ...like... them.
New eugenics:
parents leave nothing to chance.

Knowing how to read
replaced with:

knowing Excel
and Python.

The serpent wears a coat.
No more slithering to bite the unaware,
upright,
in full view,
forked tongues,
make the grade.
Engineering unfinished roads,
leaving potholes,
to gasoline addicts.

Endless screens and screams:
We are less than human now.

More tempted than not,
camels line up to enter the
eye of the needle.

Rivers run dry,
no more
baptismal water.

Bloated whales stuck sick,
like upturned forgotten goldfish.

*Cement bowls cracking
under the weight of guilt.*

Our unsatiated appetites,
for entertainment,
squeezes blood
from the lungs of gladiators,
players forget their own names.

Bees need batteries to fly,
control freaks-
making storms,

recreating a sun,
in a lab,
spitting on
Gods' plans.

Girls with ancient instructions,
bought and sold,
missing and murdered,
bordered and boundaried,
numbers replace names,
mothers have no more milk.

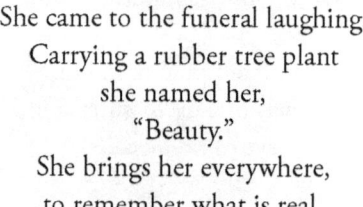

She came to the funeral laughing.
Carrying a rubber tree plant
she named her,
"Beauty."
She brings her everywhere,
to remember what is real.
Her last organic
thing.

Holding a phone to the sky,
three suns appear,
on the horizon,

reflecting,

dominoes,
lining the streets.
Dogs walk by the homeless,
wearing Ralph Lauren sweaters,
and rain boots,
scoffing soldiers,
who stare past Zombies:
worshipping the brave new world.
Millennial million heirs

have nothing to learn
or build.

Intermittently:
they eat
vegan cubes.
Some snort powder,
like a vitamin.
And drink an occasional
protein shake-
while intermittently fasting,
not to pray,
but to *ascend.*

"There are supply chain issues:"
No more food.

She places beauty in the center of a table.
The gossips gasp,

"What is SHE doing here?"

"It was HER MOTHER who died!"
retort the rebukers.

They never knew she was born.

They never played in the mud
with bare feet.

Collective tinnitus,
distracted the speaker.

*"Let's not mourn her,
let us sing."*

A clap of thunder,
sparrows shot upward,
like an exploding pen,

the ringing never ends:

you cannot ring yourself out.

Sullen silence-
broken,
with a long-forgotten hymn:

"Amazing Grace,
how sweet the sound,
that saved
a wretch,
like me,
I once
was lost
but now
I'm found
Was blind
but now,
I see."

(To pray is a punishable offense,
they sing it anyway.)

Betty's daughter
carried Beauty home,
locked the door,
to her own prison cell,
and went to bed,
because her phone said,

"Time to sleep."
She closed her eyes
and stayed awake.

The next morning,
a lip of light,
like clockwork,
birds singing,

a magnolia tree,
bloomed
over night.

Magnolia Trees and Married Farmers

The married farmers
to bed,
went cross.
After arguing over his plan
for tax evasion.

His voice thundering,
where had once been,
a long stoic silence.

Like a general,
still camped out,
knowing he's lost the war.

Awakened- the next morning,
soft pink light,
a fragrant breeze,
from their first date-tempted them
to stay under cover,
lingering longer than usual,
hands sliding over hills,
of forgone flesh,
tilled by time.

The sun
revealed the young,
blushing dawn.

The lawn ablaze,
life bursting,
the glowing orb-the glassblower's dream,
hanging off the end
of the pipe.

Fading fallen blossoms,
a candlelit chandelier,
for a daytime ball

for faeries
of forgotten futures.
Birds in finest threads,
adorn Branches,
optimistically,
beckoning
billowing clouds,
pillows for
sparrows and hawks.

Forgetting taxes and elections,
murders and deceptions,
inflation and recessions-

the farmers rise,
steady as the brook,
delivering rainbow trout,
iridescent speckles,
hinting,
glinting,
at the greater mystery-
between them.

Time stands as still
as the magnolia tree,
time speeds by,
like water that breaks the beavers' dam,
every spring,
assisted by melting ice caps,
they have only heard about,
just North,
of the bend,
in the road, in Winter.

The tree undresses
before them,
like prayer.
Her petals
fall to the wind,

draping the ground,
a blanket,
threadbare,
as her grandmother's
Antique Drunkard
patterned quilt,
stolen by the magpies-
who dragged her name
through the mud.

She shows her boughs,
like gnarled
worked arms
and hands,
reaching toward
each other,
toward the sky,
tired legs sink,
into the earth,
rooted in history.

The magnificent Magnolia,
erasing trauma and toil,
love blooms eternal,
for farmers,
who hold court,
for her majesty,
in May,
after May,
after May.

Hiraku

We gather
moving together
differently
Kayaking the narrow thread of light,
forgetting memories.
Re-membering what we forget.

Light shaft,
a sword,
pierces the canopy.
Swollen clouds,
pregnant with grief.
Rain crying,
"More thunder!"

We clap away fear,
and terrible angels.
We annihilate death,
every-time we smile,
or sing.

Four Corners

Dedicated to the life and work and friendship
of my AIM brother, spiritual advisor, and close friend,
Lenny.

Before there were
Four Corners
There was open land
s p a c e for
relationships. Nothing owned,
no lines in our sand.

The last breath
of the speechless,
before firing squads,
is always
the purest air.

Like rainstorms,
lightening cracks over
four Sacred Mountains,
ferocious poems
stories strike,
from the fallen
tortured,
and forgotten.

Cactuses flower,
in desperate places,
re-flourishing,
renewed,
squash blossoms again,

occupied land,
bodies,
minds,
souls,
mined for truth
stolen

114

reclaimed and renamed.

Shorn shores

Torn
from the tattered edges
of Earth

At the four corners
a cauldron of children
screaming for home
can be heard
where homes burned
sold
auctioned
foreclosed
names changed
rearranged

Maps laid over once
open space
parking lots
cover the mass graves
of restless ancestors
murderers
unmasked
once hidden
behind
cloth and crosses,

sleepwalking,
Changing Woman
calls for ceremony
the night chant
fills the sky.

Lost babies
find their way back
Grandparents

wait for them
at the edges of traditional
prayer songs
and hogans.

Genocide is a machine
with a voracious appetite
for the gentle
The kind
the generous
patient
and humble.
Truth tellers,
storytellers,
and pipe carriers.

Like butterflies
to the sawmill
air sucked their wings
into the teeth,
of the steel beasts.

Across the street:
the racist
trading post operator-
sells glue and spray paint
to young warriors,
so they can't fight or fly.

He forgot:
they know how to paint, to heal.

"Chief"
tells him:
"Stop! Stop selling glue to our youth!"
So the operator
went on a character
assassination mission.
What he failed to realize:

you cannot grasp
and hold the healing water:

Tó éí iiná,

those anointed:
can never be defeated.

"The Chief"
went on to
liberate the ones in prisons.
He brought them
pipe ceremonies
sweat lodges
and prayers
behind bars.

How many prisoners
were released
is unknown.
So many children
saved
by His grace.
He walked in
and gave them
the keys.

Those sentenced to death:
become stars,
a garland
a necklace of light
for the night,
they hear
Changing Woman
singing
their victory songs
around the fire.

Barbed wire

fences
lines in the skin
of our mother,

Temporary tattoos,
cannot divide
the hearts
of those who pray
for the taken,
the forsaken,
the abducted,
and the lost.

All we must hear,
is the sound
of the truth,
in a song,
in a drum,
in a prayer,
in our first language.

We hear the language
of our mother
and we are

FREE.

All machines rust,
our prayers are
invincible.

Smoke to wind
wind to stars-
We rise
We dance
We sing
We pray
Together.
Ahó!

The Day John Trudell Showed Up In My Spotify

In memory of John Trudell

"Undercurrent..."

I was sleeping my way
through work and play - my heart
already
given away,
keeping those more
local
far at bay.

He came to me
right through
Sony headphones,
he found me sitting all alone.
My heart in pieces,
having been shown,

my dreams
I'm dreaming
Just for me.
The thief is stealing
because he can't be,
feeling and reeling
with me
or having fun,

John Trudell
rode in,
with a blazing gun,
his pen,
to show me when,
he wrote the words
to all his songs,
he knew my future,
in his head.
He knew there would

come a day
when he'd record,
all we want said:

By unrequited love,
love gone astray,
about disappearing rivers,
why they couldn't stay-

*"A reappearing familiar
weaving heartbeat
into light..."*

He showed up when
I had given up,
on knowing
learning
or growing up.

And now I know
what silver hair is for:
to show the others,
I've been here before.

Before your laughter,
or your pain,
your shiny gold,
is no poor man's gain.
my wealth is
soaking
in the pouring rain.

John Trudell showed up
Saying "Hoka!"
"Yupo!"

"Time to get up!"
The world is waiting
at your door,

you,
the good girl
whose never sure,
if she is loved,
or left for dead,
at the crossroads,
where the ancestors
bled:
Sharing their wisdom
through the veiled gate,

Don't worry daughter,
it's never too late.

"Maybe that's what souls are for:
To take the hurt the heart
can't take."-John Trudell

3 Wishes

"Can I tell you,
my wishes?"
I have but three:

If I could be young again,
not so much pretty,
but brave.

Not so obedient,
I'd misbehave

I'd meet you at age 10,
we would play
in the brook.
You would give me
a toy train,
I would give you a book.

Then one day at 12,
you would ask for a kiss,
I would smile say "no!"
And run away,
into the mist!

I'd watch you pitch
in the Saturday game.
I'd ride to the field,
and watch through the fence,
while you pitched
a no hitter,
and wink
from the bench.

The second wish is simply:

To meet you again.
By chance,

and by fortune,
in a sudden Spring wind.
We would turn into each other,
and say with great joy!

"It's you! How are you doing?
Fancy meeting again!"

We would be at school,
you ask me to dance,
at a party with Chicanos,
where we plan to work,
for freedom
and justice together,
on the picket fence.
We decide to take the ride,
that tender chance,
at romance.

The last wish is a refrain:

I stay with you then.
So you'd kiss me,
and keep me
and we remember when:
You gave me a toy train,
and I gave you a book.

You'd pull out a page
and say,
with a loving look;

"I kept it in case
I found you at last!
to read you these words,
written long in the past,
by survivors
who thought,
each breath

was their last.

Until one strange,
fateful day,
prisoners pardoned,
set free,
they locked arms,
embraced,
and swam in the sea.

The lovers had found
Each-other,
in sweet destiny."

Now I want you to know,
though spread out in age,
and wishes are silly,
but fun,
a daydream,
with sage,
with no end
to dreaming,
of a beautiful stage,
where we write the lines,
of our imagined play:

With a happier ending,
for you
and for me.

Wrapped in the trust
of this love,
eternally.

Where you can be you,
and I can be me,
equaling: "we,"
we pray together,
in the way of beauty.

Where trust is ensured,
an unbroken bond-
sublime-
Protected and treasured
in a place beyond time.

Working With a Happy Broken Heart

Grateful heart is:
a full moon,
a luminous lake.

Sometimes breaking,
like the split
scorched Earth.

Memory is:
morning mist.

Sweetgrass
wears
diamonds.
Gifts from
the certain
Sun.

Light bursts forth:
trees' eyes,
greeting sunrise,
we offer corn pollen,
realize.

Four directions,
sending prayers,
westward,
wayward,
on the wind.

Hawk soars through,
your sweat lodge door,
entering your song.

Nations praying,
heal,
hope restored,

sacred hoop
renewed,
long teary river
sings again- gliding along,
alone together,
rocks are blessings
on your shore.

The beauty way prayer
lifts,
upward,
gentle,

trails of smoke-
Juniper and
Sage,
decorate the way,
altars,
for tired feet,
for those
who stay.

Tobacco offerings,
to your outstretched
hand - listening to the bones,
of our grandmothers,
who understand - the hard working,
always bear,
a shattered soul,
they all share,
a begging bowl,
and losses buried
underground.

Tightrope walking,
between
life and death,
grandfather knows,

destiny's plan,
sprinkling stars,
across the land.

Night
a shawl,
for changing woman,
woven by our mother's
hands-

Some flights,
aren't taken-
tomorrow's sand.

Sundancer,
will you dance
a prayer with me?

Sacred,
each journey,
we finally see:
medicine missed,
while lost at sea.

Now we are,
washed up,
on the beach,
polished by,
punishing waves,
happy-
no more aching,
no more need.

Longing for nothing,
the river-edged
sword
is sure,
here to give,
we

must endure-
the gifts
we have,
turn around,
and ask,

"Will you surrender to love?
Can we share peace, at last?"

Deer at Dawn

In memory, for Josh Desmarais

I found the deer
at dawn today,
and think
they must have dreamt-
of humanity
who found their way,
and eased their sad lament.

For innocence consumed them,
in a raging forest fire.
Desire fed,
the canopy doomed,
last bird on a wire.

A bed was sewn,
with golden thread,
laced with morning dew
the dampness
of the walking dead,
A buck chased a doe
She knew.

The dream,
she screamed,
to the hunter's screen-
"put down the unholy guns!"

The spirit chaser
who seeks meat
that's lean
knows
we are the only ones.

We keep keen watch,
on earth's affairs-
it is man

130

who walks remiss.
Like captured wild mustang mares,
In prisons enshrouded by mist.

As sure as leaves fall,
from autumn trees,
and winter wears a coat,
of snowy mountain's majesties,
Spring comes to get her goat.

The dreaming deer know
the hunter's fear,
to horizon's edge they run.
As soon as the bullet draws
death too near,
she bows to the rising Sun.

She also sees the truer time
will come,
When guns are firing like pistons-
everything has come undone,
humanity will bend her ear,
finally,
she will listen:

To the graceful calling of the deer,
who whisper to her at dawn-
"You have nothing left to fear,
For all greed and lies are gone."

Peace

Peace is:
a voice in the wind that says,
"This way!"
Peace is a fire in the heart,
that burns,
for the cause of liberation.

It is the liquid dream of water.
Quenching our thirst
after a drought.

Peace is a night sky,
layered with stars,
thick as heavy deep snow
made of crystal
diamonds
from the sky.

Peace is a river
we can all swim in
drink from
play in...
uncontaminated
by nuclear waste,
postindustrial haste.

Peace is a smile
from a passing stranger
we know we met before.

Peace is a long hug,
from a friend,
when you stand at grief's door:
Unsure of your strength to enter.

Peace is a mentor saying.
"Well done, good work!"

When you feel too weary to go on.

Peace is being invited to sit at the table,
saying grace,
and eating in the company of family
you make,
while building your new life.

Peace.

Peace is making beauty with everyone everywhere,
In keeping with the Creator's breath,
Of life and light,
in every Magnolia blossom,
in every face,
and place.

Peace is what we share,
arms outstretched,
across great cultural,
political and
economic divides.

Peace is a dance of faith,
while some of us share a line
to be vaccinated,
uncertain and trusting,
we care.

Peace is a Sunrise,
after the long dark night of your soul,
saving you from despair.

Peace is a voice on the wind,
whispering:
"Keep going,
you're not alone."
Peace.

Is a verb,
we share.

AFTERWORD

Colonization made enemies out of my ancestors.
Decolonization made them into lovers.
Poetry exorcised the demons.
Prayer made them angels.

MEET THE AUTHOR

Jehann El-Bisi is a single mother who was trained as an elementary education specialist. Holding a Doctorate in Teacher Education and Curriculum Studies from the University of Massachusetts at Amherts, and as a survivor of trauma, she discovered the use of narrative, art, and storytelling, as powerful modalities for healing.

As a "triracial" woman of African, European and Native American descent and ancestry, she is dedicated to multicultural and inclusive literature for children and adults.